Learning to Read and Write

WENDY BODY

Longman

LONGMAN GROUP UK LIMITED
Longman House
Burnt Mill, Harlow, Essex CM20 2JE, England
and Associated Companies throughout the World

First published 1989
ISBN 0 582 03814 6

Set in 10/11 Syntax, Linotype

Printed and bound in Great Britain by
Courier International Ltd, Tiptree, Essex

Contents

Introduction

Dear Parents,

For the past twenty three years I have been a teacher working first of all in primary schools, then secondary and for the final sixteen years of my teaching career I have worked with teachers, pupils and parents at a Reading Centre. During that time I ran many courses for teachers and some for parents on the teaching of literacy skills. I was also an author of children's books and a consultant for educational publishers. In 1988, I gave up my job to concentrate totally on my writing, consultancy and lecturing.

I tell you all this not so you can work out how old I am (!) but to give you some idea of the kind of person who is writing this book. It is impossible to spend sixteen years of your professional life exclusively concerned with the field of children learning to read and write without developing certain beliefs.

I believe very strongly that to be literate, to be able to read and write, is one of the most important things we can learn. It gives us access to the minds, emotions and development of the rest of mankind; it runs from Shakespeare to shopping lists, from Barbara Taylor Bradford to DIY; for by reading we can feed our emotions, our intellect and our experience. Just think of all the occasions in your life when you read or write anything at all and then imagine how different that life would be if you could neither read nor write.

I believe, therefore, that schools have an overwhelmingly important duty to help children learn these crucial skills. Reading,

after all, is the cornerstone on which the whole of the school curriculum rests.

I know from my work with parents and the letters I receive that they too recognise the importance of learning to read and write for their children. They want to help them, but sometimes feel unsure about doing so in the first place or how they can best go about it. I have written this book to try and help you to help your child.

You can use the book in two ways. . .If you read it from cover to cover you should end up knowing quite a bit in general terms about children learning to read and write which will, in turn, make helping your child a little easier. You may, on the other hand, have certain questions or worries that you want answered, in which case you can dip into the book. I haven't been able to include every single question that parents have ever asked me, but I've covered most of them I think!

Writing a book for parents is something which I have wanted to do for several years because I believe that parents have such an important contribution to make with regard to their children's learning. I hope that you will enjoy reading it and that it will help you to support your child.

5

Take off with books

Take off with books;
Not with the rocket's roar
Take off in silence
And in fancy soar
At rocket speed
To every land and time
And see, spread out beneath,
Past, present, future
As you higher climb.
Explore those worlds
The rocket cannot reach,
Iroy, Camelot and Crusoe's lonely beach.
No path forbid, no darkling secret hid;
Books reached the moon
Before real rockets did.

Ogden Nash

What we want for our children
is literacy . . .
that power over print which will
help them to explore and enjoy
their living, their heritage, their history
and their future.
What we want for our children
is a key . . .
a key to the world of the written word
wherein all human life, knowledge
and emotion are waiting . . .

Wendy Body

LEARNING TO READ AND WRITE

It could be said that there are two main aspects to reading: word recognition and comprehension – knowing what words 'say' and understanding them. But these two aspects must go hand in hand for reading is all about making meaning. An author has a message for the readers and readers have to work out or reconstruct the meanings which the author had in mind when his or her thoughts were first translated into written words. When we've done that we can say that we have understood what we have read or reconstructed the author's message. For reading is *not* simply about translating print into speech. Being able to see the word 'cat' and then pronouncing it correctly is not much use unless the reader understands the concept of cat and knows what it means. Without this understanding, reading is only making noises or what has often been called 'barking at print' – something to be avoided at all costs if a reader is to make progress!

So what does a child have to learn in order to begin reading? Well, before reading comes learning to speak; as they learn to talk children are learning about language and the way it hangs together and makes sense. They learn that we don't say things like: "I to the shops will go tomorrow." They couldn't tell you *why* we don't say it, they just know it!

Children already know a great deal about language when they come to learn to read but spoken language and written language are different as well as similar, so they have to learn other important things as well. They have to learn that:

- Print consists of a 'message'. It tells you things and it makes sense and it is the print in a book which tells us what to say and not the pictures.
- We read English print in a certain direction – from top to bottom of a page, from left to right along a line and

by turning pages in a front to back direction through a book.

- Print is made up of words and letters.

There are some difficult things for children to learn here. For example: in talking, children are not aware of words as separate units – 'jelly and icecream' sounds like one thing when a child says it; whereas in print, of course, it is three distinct units. So children have to learn to match the words they are *saying* with the number of words they are *seeing*.

Again, in their everyday learning, children have discovered that objects don't change their identities if you look at them from different angles – teddy bears and teacups are still teddy bears and teacups whether or not they are turned around up upside down! This doesn't apply to some letters however (think about bpd or nu) and it is one reason why young children commonly reverse or confuse certain letters.

How *do* children learn these things? Well, they don't learn them simply by being told! They learn them by example – through sharing books with adults (one reason why it's so important for you to share books with your young child), by copying the reading behaviour of adults, and by experience.

What does happen when we read?

Huge sums of money and countless hours of time have been spent in trying to research what goes on in our brains when we read and how we learned to do it in the first place. The human brain is so amazingly complex that we still don't fully know the answer to the question. We have a pretty good idea about most aspects, however, and we know (or believe!) that what follows is a major part.

Memory is obviously important in lots of ways; for example, it helps us to recognise words and enables us to keep in mind what has gone before when we read so that we can make sense of something as a whole. We also know that readers use three sources of information or knowledge when they are dealing with print. They have technical names which you may be interested in knowing and are:

Semantic Anything to do with meaning, meaning within a text and what could loosely be called the reader's 'sense-making machinery' brought to bear on a text or piece of writing. This comes from experience of living and making sense of our surroundings and in turn, helps the reader to make a text make sense.

Syntactic The knowledge all readers have (mainly because they can speak) of the patterns and structure of the language – the way words can be linked together to make meaningful sentences and phrases,

n other words their grammatical knowledge.

Grapho-phonic The sound-symbol system of the language – knowing that certain groups of letters are likely to be pronounced in a certain way (*ing* in string, for example.)

These three kinds of knowledge and information seem to be used almost simultaneously. We don't, for instance, look at the letters within a word then check to see if we can pronounce them before deciding if a word makes sense within whatever we are reading. We don't, however, have to look at every single letter in a word – we usually don't need to.

Let's see how this might work in practice. . .In the sentence *He tied it up with* _____, we can make a very good guess at what the missing word is from our knowledge of the way sentences are constructed, (our grammatical knowledge tells us that the word couldn't be *slowly*, for example); and the general meaning of the sentence together with what we already know about such things means that the word couldn't be *water*! If we have a bit more information, such as the word begins with *str* we can be pretty certain as to what this missing word is and we don't need to see the rest of its letters.

When we read, of course, all these things are happening every split second and we are simply not aware of what we are doing unless, perhaps, we meet a totally unfamiliar word and then we slow right down and puzzle it out (or skip it)!

Learning to read is not something which finishes as soon as children can read quite difficult stories with understanding, expression and enjoyment. They need to go on learning various things and refining their reading if they are to use reading as a means of learning. For example, they need to learn:

- how to select appropriate books to find out about something;

- how to use an index or a list of contents;
- to be able to adjust their reading speed and style of reading to suit the demands of a particular text. (You read your bedtime novel in a very different way from that in which you read your tax return, for example.)

The early primary years are a crucial and important time for developing reading skills but it is worth remembering that the process of becoming an efficient reader is one that continues throughout and well beyond the primary years. What's happening in primary schools today as far as reading is concerned? There are those who might say 'not enough' when we hear about teenagers and adults who have spent a good few years in school and who still can't read or write well. There are many reasons why some people have problems with the written word and you will find something about this later on in the book. For now, let's concentrate on what schools are doing!

Teaching reading in school

Parents can easily be confused by what appear to be several very different approaches to the teaching of reading in primary schools today. This section is intended to give you some idea of various approaches which may be used so that you are better able to assess what is happening in your child's school or prospective school.

First of all, there are three important things to bear in mind:

1 Teachers want to do the best for their pupils and recognise the importance of learning to read in the early years.
2 There is no evidence at all to prove that any one approach is better than another for all children. Many schools use a variety or combination of approaches so that they can best meet the needs of all their pupils.

3 The teaching of reading has changed somewhat in the last ten years or so. You are very likely, therefore, to find some differences between the way that you remember learning to read and the way that your child is taught today. It might be the case that you can't remember very much about the way you were taught to read. This is quite common; unless they had problems with reading as a child, all that most adults can remember are two things – the time when they couldn't read and then when they could!

Organisational approaches to teaching reading

Broadly speaking there are three – which are not in order of importance, rather that the first is the least common and the third probably the most common.

The apprenticeship approach to reading

This is used by a minority of schools and it is often linked with what is called a 'Real Books' approach. It has the following features:

- Reading schemes are not used at all. Instead the school has a wide variety of story and information books which include books like *Picture Puffins*. This is why the term 'Real Books' is used i.e. books that are not from a reading scheme.
- Children are given a completely free choice to select the books which they want to read. It doesn't matter if a book is too difficult for them to read alone because it will be used with support.
- The child learns to read a book by sharing it with an adult and by reading it over several times – which she or he will want to do because it is a book which they have chosen in the first place.

● It is the adult who is giving the child the model of how to read – hence the name 'Apprenticeship Approach' with its idea of the novice learning by the side of the skilled craftsman or woman.

This approach demands a great deal of teachers and it is not easy to ensure that in an average-sized class every child will receive the required amount of support. This is probably the reason why it is not favoured by too many infant teachers at the moment. Those schools that do work in this way do so because they see this as the most natural way of learning to read and because, they argue, reading schemes not only encourage competitiveness but also do not offer books of high enough quality to make children into lovers of books as well as technically proficient readers.

Using a graded collection of books

This has the following main features:

● A wide variety of books are used which will probably include books from some reading schemes.
● The books are grouped into several stages of difficulty e.g. books with no text, books with single words or captions and so on. There are sources of guidance to advise teachers on the reading levels of many published books (largely educational series) available from The Reading and Language Information Centre at Reading University, for example.
● Nearly always, the books are coded with coloured sticky labels to show which level or stage they are at.

- Children choose books from within the level which is most appropriate to their stage of reading development. They can, however, choose easier or harder books as well as they progress through the stages or levels.

This approach, often called 'Individualised Reading', like the previous one arose some years ago as a result of dissatisfaction with the then available reading schemes, together with a desire to ensure that children had access to a wide variety of books in order to help develop a love of reading.

Reading schemes

Schools use reading schemes in a variety of ways:

- having one scheme as the sole source of books in the early stages of learning to read;
- using one scheme as the core of the reading programme but giving children the opportunity to read many other books as well – these may well be grouped or coded into levels which correspond to those of the scheme;
- having a mixture of several schemes available so that teachers can choose the scheme they feel to be most suitable for a child or group of children.

Teachers use reading schemes because they offer them a structure in which to work,

they have the benefit of support materials, e.g. workbooks, games, teacher's books and they can help to ensure some continuity throughout the school. Schemes, however they are used, are a popular feature of the teaching of reading. The best reading schemes tend, with a couple of exceptions from amongst the older ones, to be the more recently published examples and they are very different from the schemes of years ago. Those were rightly criticised as being too narrow and restricting, offering books which were not proper stories, written in rather strange language and portraying characters and social situations which are out of step with the real world. Recent schemes have changed all that and the best offer books which are visually appealing, written in a natural language style and have stories which children love.

There are over twenty reading schemes available. There is not room to list them all so I will mention only the recent and the older but still very popular ones.

It may well be that your child's school or prospective school is using one or some of these particular schemes. Do ask if you can see any scheme that your child may be using – it's always good to be a little familiar with, for example, the characters she or he will be reading about.

Whatever approach a school has to organising it's books, it is quite possible that there will be a school library in addition to

Scheme	Main Author(s)	First published
Reading World	Pat Edwards & Wendy Body	Longman, 1987
New Way	Various	Macmillan, 1987
Sunshine	June Melser	Heinemann, 1987
The Reading Tree	Rod Hunt	OUP, 1986
Open Door	Elizabeth Lawrence & Noreen Wetton	Nelson, 1986
Storychest	June Melser & Joy Cowley	Arnold-Wheaton, 1982
Reading 360	Various	Ginn, 1978
Breakthrough to Literacy	Mackay, Thompson & Schaub	Longman, 1970
One, Two, Three & Away!	Sheila McCullagh	Collins, 1964

Child using Storychest book

Child using Longman Reading World book

any classroom collections of books. The school library may be used by even the youngest children to help them learn about using books as a source of information as well as a source of recreation. Sadly, there are quite a few Infant schools which do not have a school library. This is not because they do not recognise its value, rather that they do not have an extra classroom where it could be housed.

Teaching approaches and considerations

A school may use one, a combination or all of the following:

Shared reading

Large format or oversized books are read by a small group with the teacher. The teacher will use the book in much the same way as is described in the diagram.

The books may be specially published ones (some of the recently published

Shared reading

Reading to children: can they . . ./do they . . .

- re-tell the story?
- relate what they have heard to their own experiences?
- describe what is happening in the illustrations?
- know the direction in which pages are turned?
- understand that you read the words, not the pictures?
- understand what is meant by *page, word, line, turn over,* etc.?
- appreciate that you start in a certain place and read the print in a certain direction?
- hear differences and similarities between words?
- on re-readings, join in or 'echo-read' parts, such as phrases that are repeated?
- given one word, find another like it on the page?
- notice and remark on visual details in words?
- listen to, enjoy and follow the story?

Reading preparation – taken from Longman Reading World Teachers' Book

reading schemes have big books of one sort or another, as well) or home-made ones which the teacher and children have made together. The sharing of any book by an adult with a child – in the classroom or at home – where both are reading is also described as shared reading.

Phonics

This is where a child is taught to use the sounds and patterns of letters in order to help them deal with unfamiliar words. Some teachers believe that while all children need some knowledge of letter patterns and sounds, they should not be encouraged to 'sound out' or 'build up' words; rather that they should use their phonic knowledge to help them guess what words are likely to be and then to check their guesses. Other teachers believe that sounding out words is helpful. For example, faced with the word *sheep* a child may be encouraged to break the word into parts, sound them out and then put them together. To do this he or she must know how *sh, ee* and *p* are commonly pronounced and how to blend the sounds together to make the word.

Schools using this kind of approach will

probably have a definite phonics teaching programme which the children follow, for example:

Single consonants: b c d f g h j k l m n p etc.
'Short' vowel sounds: a (cat) e (egg) i (ink) o (fox) u (up)
Consonant blends: br cr sn fl st gl sw str etc.
Consonant digraphs: ch (church) sh th (thin, then) ph
'Long' vowel sounds: ee (feet) ai (rain) u-e (tube) etc.
and so on. . .

Other schools will have a much 'looser' approach because they are treating phonic knowledge as something which is best acquired incidentally. They believe that it is not helpful to teach children to be over-reliant on the use of phonics because there are so many exceptions to the 'rules' which children are sometimes taught. Think about words like *done, put, women, walk, half,* or *one,* for example. They also recognise that phonics learning or a phonic approach to reading is very hard for some children; it requires the ability to distinguish between various sounds and then relate them to a particular visual pattern which must be learned. It's easy to use phonics to sound out a word when you know what that word says already, but with a quite unfamiliar word there could be more than one way of pronouncing it. For example, how do you pronounce *read* or *bow*? You need the rest of the sentence to help you as in "She's got several strings to her bow."

Phonic skills and knowing about the sound-symbol system of the language do have to be acquired by the reader, as I said earlier. The debate in schools is about how much emphasis to give it and the best way of helping children. For example: showing children a list of words which they know already such as *shop*, *shell*, *she* and *shoe* and talking about a common pattern in them is very different from giving the two letters in isolation and teaching that they make a 'sh' sound.

Before we leave phonics for the moment, it is worth pointing out that many children learn to read without any phonic instruction at all – they acquire the necessary knowledge for themselves through the course of their reading.

Developing a sight vocabulary

When teachers talk about this they mean those words which a child can recognise instantly without having to work at them in any way. Children find some words much easier to learn/remember than others, especially the words which have been described as 'personal, private and picturesque' – a child's own name or words like *elephant* or *dinosaur* or *Wow*.

It is the words like *was*, *they*, *who*, etc. which they find more difficult because these words are more abstract or shorter and so easier to confuse. Unfortunately, it is words like these which are so important because they make up so much of written language! This is why they are referred to as 'Key' or 'High Frequency' or 'Heavy Duty' words. Did you know for instance, that the following words make up 25% of *all* reading – *a and he I in is it of that the to was*? That's pretty amazing, isn't it?

Comprehension

All teachers want to ensure that when children read they do so with understanding as well as being able to pronounce the words and read with some flow and expression. Being able to read the words and sentences aloud without comprehending what they are about is simply not enough. You could read the following sentence but there's not a lot of point in being able to read it because it doesn't make sense! Try it though. . .

One spling feng the woggit stracked its buncle.

You can even read this sentence with some expression so that it *sounds* as if it makes sense to you when of course it doesn't. Children can do this when they are reading aloud and so teachers want to make sure that they are getting sense and meaning from their readings.

You might think teachers could check this simply by asking questions, but that isn't always enough. Having read that sentence about the woggit can you answer this question correctly? (Look back if you need to!)

What did the woggit strack?

Yes, of course you were able to get it right! The question only requires that you give back the words used in the sentence, what is called the literal meaning. If, however, you had been asked to draw a buncle you wouldn't be able to – which shows you don't understand what it is all about!

It is important not only that children do understand the literal meaning of what they read but also that they can infer things from print. For example: "The crisp morning air made her face tingle." The inference, although the sentence doesn't actually say so, is that it was cold – something which a child would need to understand if the sentence was in a story that was being read. Teachers will use a range of techniques, in addition to questions, to check and develop children's understanding of what they read, for example:

- drawing some detail from a story;
- putting individual sentences or pictures into the correct sequence of events;
- filling in the words where gaps have been left in a sentence;
- asking a child to re-tell a story in his/her own words.

Assessing reading and reading ages

There are two ways of assessing reading and these are called *Informal* and *Formal*.

Informal assessment Every time teachers listen to children reading they are making some assessment of their progress and watching to see how the reading skills are developing. From time to time they may ask children to read with no help and take a closer and very detailed look at what mistakes a child is making and how they go about dealing with unfamiliar words. From this kind of detailed study of children's

reading, teachers can see what particular aspects of an individual's reading need working on. For example, a child may constantly misread words like *they* and *were* which would suggest that some further work on high frequency words is needed – using some worksheets or reading games, for instance. Informal assessment is ongoing – not something which is only done once or twice a year. It is called informal assessment because the teacher uses the ordinary classroom materials and because it is done in an informal way – the children will not realise they are being tested.

Formal assessment As the name implies, this is a much more formal process – children are given reading tests under test conditions. Formal testing of this sort is not used a great deal in Infant schools; the most likely use will be in the case of children who are having problems and children at the end of their first two years in school or at the age of transfer to the Junior department or

school. Of course, there are schools who use reading tests more frequently than others.

There are a large number of reading tests which are available for school use and most of them involve children reading either single words or sentences/passages. When a test is marked, the score is translated into a reading quotient or a reading age. As far as reading quotients are concerned, below 85 is below average, 85–115 is average and over 115 is above average. More commonly, a child's test score is translated into an age equivalent score – a reading age. The idea here is that a seven year old child who has a reading age of 8 years 6 months is said to have scored at the level which could be expected from the average eight and a half year old *but. . .*

Never place too much reliance on a supposed reading age for your child for the following reasons:

- Reading tests can never measure a child's total reading ability; they can only test aspects of it. A word recognition test (reading a list of single words) can only test a child's ability to read words in isolation, for example. This, incidentally, is the hardest thing to do because the child does not have the benefit of the rest of the words in a sentence to help in working out a word she or he may not be sure of.
- Reading tests vary enormously in their results; the same child given two different tests could have two different reading ages which could vary by a year or eighteen months.
- All we can ever say with certainty is that a particular child has a particular reading age as measured by a particular reading test on a particular date. Another day and another test and it could be a very different story.

Used properly, reading tests do have some value for teachers. Many teachers are, however, reluctant to talk about test results

and reading ages to parents for the reasons I have mentioned above and for fear that a parent might consider the child's reading age as a fixed and gospel thing (or even worse, that they might tell their child which might lead to all kinds of misperceptions about his or her ability on the child's part.)

We cannot leave the subject of assessment without some brief mention of the new 1988 Education Reform Act. A feature of this Act of Parliament is that for the main or core subject areas, including English or Language teaching, there will be broad programmes of study for all teachers to follow at all stages of schooling. There will also be attainment targets to aim for and children will be assessed at 7 and 11 in the Primary school. Teachers will be assessing children at other stages as well, of course, but these two ages are the important ones – the reporting ages as they are called. It seems likely that as far as reading and writing are concerned, most of the primary school assessments will be of things which are done as part of the everyday, 'normal' classroom activity. These developments are some way off yet and, at the time of writing this book, we do not know for certain any details; the various working groups are still making their reports to the government who will then make their decisions. Watch the newspapers for further information!

Reading activities

There are many things which happen in a primary classroom which are all essential aspects of 'the reading programme' and a child's reading instruction. Here are just a few examples:

- reading to the teacher from a reading book;
- sharing a big book with the teacher and other children;
- reading instructions – to make a simple model, for example;
- listening to stories on tape or read aloud by the teacher;

- sorting pictures into groups according to their first letter sounds;
- putting individual sentences into a sequence of events;
- playing reading games to develop or practise some particular skill e.g. Bingo with words instead of numbers;
- matching pictures with words or with sentences;
- reading and perhaps learning songs, poems, rhymes or hymns;
- finding a book on a particular topic in the library or book corner.

So next time you ask your child if she or he has done any reading in school today and the answer is 'no' – don't believe it! One way or another, a lot of what is happening during the school day is linked with developing reading skills – even though children themselves may not realise it!

Finding out more about a school's approach to reading

Hopefully, if your child is already at a particular school you will know most of this already but it may help you in the situation of having to assess one or more prospective schools.

First of all there are some questions you might ask of a Headteacher. . .

1 "Do you use a reading scheme or an individualised reading approach?"
   If the answer is 'a scheme' ask about it and find out if there was any particular reason for choosing/using it. Don't be afraid to ask what other books your child would be reading as well.
2 "Please could you tell me what other

things the children do as part of the reading programme. . . do they have any phonics teaching, for example?''

3 ''Is there a school library? Please would it be possible for me to have a look at it?'' (Look for lots of attractively displayed books and a generally inviting air to the room/area with places for children to browse comfortably.)

4 ''Is there anything in particular you like parents to do to help their child's reading?''

Obviously, these are starter questions and you may well find that all this information is given without you having to ask. As a Head or teacher is talking, you'll find that other questions will arise naturally and don't forget that one of the best ways of getting more information out of someone is to say something like: ''That sounds interesting – could you tell me a little more about it, please?''

Whatever the particular approach to teaching reading in a primary school, there are various points to notice about the general environment which will give you a good idea of whether or not a school really is aiming to encourage a 'Reading is an important and worthwhile activity' attitude amongst the children. For example, look for:

- A good number of books which are well displayed – in the classroom, library or other areas of the school – with at least some of the covers facing outwards to make the books more inviting for children.

- Books that are in a reasonable condition. This is a tricky one; in these days of financial constraints it *is* hard for schools to replace books to the degree which they might wish, but a book stock which is totally composed of dirty, scruffy and dog-eared books is hardly likely to appeal to children and make them *want* to read.

However the books are displayed or housed and however poorly off for

books a school might be, there is no excuse for seeing books left lying on the floor or in a generally very untidy state. It suggests that a school is not doing all that it might to teach children to value and care for books.

- Posters/pictures and displays of work which are linked to books and reading.

- In general terms, book areas which appear inviting to you; if they don't make *you* feel that you'd like to go and have a closer look then it is unlikely that they will be very appealing to children.

What is involved in learning to write?

As you might expect, writing, like reading, has close links with speaking – very young children soon learn that things can be written as well as said. Before they can read, most young children will 'write' – not in any conventional sense because they don't know what to do to begin with! They are very curious about the whole business and if they see a parent writing something they usually want to know what mummy or daddy is doing and if they can do it too.

There are very definite stages which children go through in the process of learning to write – and at each stage they are convinced that they are writing properly! They move from random scribble and scribble in lines to letter-like shapes and patterns which are set out in a line like real writing. Gradually, 'proper' letters begin to emerge as the child tries writing words –not usually recognisable as such!

There are important things which need to be learned about writing:

- Writing is another way of saying something; we write for lots of different reasons which usually involve the need to remember or record something and the need to communicate with people not in a face to face situation with us.

- Writing in English means using

combinations of letters to represent the sounds and words of the language in their standard and generally accepted forms i.e. letters are put together to make words which have commonly accepted spellings.

- English writing follows a left to right line across a page and top to bottom down the page direction. (Other languages e.g. Chinese, follow different lines and directions.)
- We use additional marks to divide, add meaning or emphasis to writing – punctuation. Some of these are used all the time e.g. full stops, commas, speech and question marks whereas others such as colons and semi colons are used less frequently.
- We use different styles of writing for different purposes – a letter for a job application is in a very different style from that of one written to an old and close friend, for example.

Perhaps even more than reading, learning to write is a continual process which spans many years. The first three things a child has to learn about writing are:

- that it is a way of communication;
- that it follows a certain direction;
- how to form letters.

In order to begin to learn how to form letters a child must first be able to control the pencil, which in turn means a reasonable level of *fine motor control*. We describe anything to do with moving our bodies as motor skills. Gross motor skills would be, for example, running, jumping, kicking, hopping. Fine motor skills are needed for using scissors, drawing or writing, for example – actions which require smaller and more controlled movements of the hand. As you have watched your young child growing up so you will have seen the growing ability to control movements and manipulate smaller objects. You will probably have noticed that there is a period when young children use either their left or right hand equally happily. Gradually, one is preferred more than the other and it is at this stage that a child shows whether he or she will be right or left-handed.

This 'handedness' can take a long while to become established in some children and you should *never* try to make your child use one hand in preference to the other. Neither should you worry if your child appears to be neither right nor left-handed by the time she or he goes to school – this is not at all uncommon.

Learning to write at school

Teachers will be using all kinds of ways to get children involved in writing and to make sure that they do appreciate the communication and direction aspects mentioned earlier. They will, for example, invite a child to talk about a picture she or he has drawn and they will write what the child says on the picture. Soon the child will be writing over the teacher's writing or copying underneath it. They may ask children to write so that they can see whether or not they know anything about writing. Are children scribbling, using letter-like shapes and so on?

Some schools use *Breakthrough to Literacy* (published by Longman) to help start their children off. A card called a Sentence Maker has lots of separate words slotted into it. The child uses these words to make up his or her own sentences by placing them in a special stand. When the child has composed the sentence (using additional words written on blank cards by the teacher if the child doesn't have the word she or he wants in the folder) it is then copied into a book. This approach means that the child can concentrate on composing without having to worry about spelling and handwriting at the same time – something which is extremely hard for children in the first stages of learning to write.

2

Child using the Breakthrough to Literacy Sentence Maker

Pencil grip

Whatever the approach to writing, all teachers are concerned to teach children the correct formation of letters and a good pencil grip as soon as possible. The drawing will show you which is the best pencil grip for both left and right-handed children to use. It is the best because it is the one which children are likely to find the most comfortable when they eventually need to do quite a lot of writing.

Letter formation

There is bound to be some variation in the letter shapes which the children are taught between various schools so it is important to find out which style your child will be taught if you wish to help at home. A few

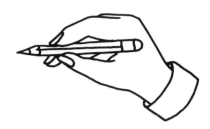

Pencil grips for right-and left-handed children

schools teach children a joined-up style of writing right from the start; most, however will teach one of the following styles – both using the lower case forms of the letters to begin with rather than capital letters. (So please don't ever teach your child to write using block capitals e.g. MANDY WENT TO THE SHOPS.)

There is a growing trend to teach the second style which differs from the first only in that letters ending in a downwards stroke have a small tail or serif added to

Style 1

Style 2

them. The reason for teaching this style is that it makes the development of a joined handwriting style easier for the child later on. Instead of having to go through three stages of learning:

from *man* to *man* to *man* ;

the child has only two:

from *man* to *man* .

Teaching a 'd' with a serif on it also has the advantage of making it look like a slightly different shape from a b – and we all know how easy it is for children to confuse those two letters!

Learning about the process of writing

Children do a vast amount of writing during their years at school and it is by *actually* writing that they learn to develop their skills. There is a growing change of emphasis in primary schools which has arisen over the last couple of years as a result of greater insights into the way children can be helped to develop their writing skills. There has, for example, been The National Writing Project which has involved hundreds of teachers in examining and finding ways of learning to write which are an improvement on what has previously been done in the majority of schools. (Education, like many other areas of life, does benefit from new ideas and tried and tested research!)

What is happening now is that children are being taught what is often called a 'Process' approach to writing. Just stop and think for a minute about how you might tackle a piece of writing such as a letter to your bank manager or a special report for your boss. You would probably go through the following steps:

- think about what you want to say;
- write a rough copy;
- check to see if you've left out anything

important or if you've phrased things badly;
- check on any spellings you aren't sure about and the punctuation;
- write/type a final version.

That, more or less, is a process approach to writing! In an increasing number of schools children are learning about writing in the following way:

Composing Children are encouraged to choose for themselves the topics they want to write about – instead of, for example, the whole class being told to write a story with the same subject. They will talk their ideas over with the teacher or with other children and be given help if necessary.

Drafting They write a first draft of their story which is then read and discussed.

Revising In the light of the child's own feelings about the writing and the comments or suggestions which have been made to her or him, changes and additions are made to the first draft.

Editing Spelling and punctuation are checked – with the help of the teacher if needed.

Final version The story is written out neatly or typed – or printed if the child has used a computer.

Publishing The children may then make a book out of the story (designing pages and the cover, doing illustrations and so on), display their work on the wall, share it with other children – in fact, make their work public in some way.

There are a few important points to make about this way of working:

- I have used the example of writing a story but the approach is used with a range of different kinds of writing in order for children to learn about writing for different purposes and in different styles. (For example: writing a report of a science experiment or writing instructions of how to make something.) Often, when a different writing style is introduced, a teacher will write with the children so giving them a model of how to do it.

- Not every piece of writing a child does has to go through all the previously mentioned steps and stages – there are still the one-off, do-it-once writing activities in the classroom. What often happens is that it is the child who makes the decision about which piece of writing out of five or so examples he or she wants to work on and take through to the publishing stage.
- Spelling and handwriting are not

something which is left to develop by chance. All children receive teaching as far as these two important aspects of writing are concerned. You will find more information about this in the questions dealing with spelling and handwriting in the second part of the book.

Parents and schools

Some years ago it used to be the case that parents were not really welcome in schools when it came to their child's education. There were actually schools which displayed notices saying 'No Parents Beyond This Point'. Thankfully, things have changed a great deal in the last ten years or

so and the general feeling now in most schools is much more one of welcoming and involving parents in what the children are doing.

Naturally, schools do and will vary with regard to how much parental involvement they encourage when it comes to children learning to read and write. Some schools invite parents into the classroom to read stories, share books or play reading games with the children. Others will ask for volunteers to help make materials for the children's use – I've seen, for example, wonderful soft toys and puppets of characters from reading schemes which have been sewn or knitted by parents.

Whatever the degree and nature of parental involvement in individual schools there is, almost certainly, the hope and expectation that parents will listen to children reading when they bring home their reading book from school. This can be a precious few minutes which is a joy to both parent and child or it can be a

nightmare! The cartoons are exaggerations, but there is an element of truth in both!

It doesn't take too much imagination to guess how mum in the first cartoon and the child in the second are both feeling – reading a school reading book is the last thing they need at that moment!

Time is a precious commodity for all of us, but the minutes you find to listen to your child reading can be minutes which will be of enormous value – short and long term. With the best will in the world, teachers cannot spend the amount of time which they would wish with each child on an individual basis – there are simply too many of them. This is one reason why they like parents to listen to reading at home.

Listening to your child read

So how can you make the best of those few minutes together with your child's reading book? Here are a few suggestions. . .

- Arrange a time when you *both* want to read. This will vary from family to family so negotiate with your child whether or not it's to be after school, after tea, before bedtime or at bedtime etc. Bedtime can have disadvantages in that a child may be too tired to read for himself and it would be better for all concerned for bedtime to be the time when a parent reads to the child.
- Sit comfortably, side by side in a room where, if possible, you can be by yourselves – without the television or radio on. This is likely to ensure that your child's attention is on the book and you rather than anything else!
- Ask what the story is about so far or, in the case of a new book, what your child thinks the story might be about. In either case, have a brief look through the pictures together before you start the reading: this serves either as a reminder of what has happened already or an introduction to the story.

- During the reading, allow the child as much time as he or she wants to look at the pictures – some children like to savour the details of illustrations before they go on to the next part. If your child is one who likes to rush on with the story and seems to be paying no attention to the pictures, encourage her or him to go back and look at them and talk about them afterwards. Questions like "Do you remember what was happening here?" can be a good way in to this. It is entirely possible that the pictures are not worth looking at which is why they were ignored in the first place! This shouldn't happen too often, but if the illustrations *are* very poor then don't bother forcing your child to discuss them! If your child does express dislike or disappointment with the pictures then it can be a good idea to ask his or her opinion of the sort of illustrations which might have been used instead – this will often lead to a purposeful re-reading of the text (good practice!) to check details of what should have been included or what might be portrayed instead.
- When your child makes a mistake and says the wrong word, wait until the end of a phrase or sentence (a natural break) to see if, by reading on a little, the child realises a mistake has been made and self-corrects it. If no attempt at self-correction is made, then intervene by saying something like: "Wait a minute, something didn't quite make sense there, did it? Let's go back and have another look. . ." Then read from the beginning of the sentence again. If your child cannot then guess the word, simply say what it is and ask him or her to read that part again before continuing.
- Sometimes children will not self-correct because the word they have substituted does makes sense – for example, reading 'mummy' instead of 'mother'. It is better not to intervene and disrupt the flow of the story when children make mistakes of this sort which do not affect the meaning of what they are reading. You can, if you wish, return to it at the end and ask the child what the word says. Often, they will read it correctly in these circumstances which is fine and the child should be praised. If, however, the error is repeated, then say something like: "That's a jolly good guess and it *does* make sense but the word is mother." You could then play 'Hunt for mother' and ask the child if they can spot the word anywhere else in the book or on the page – *if* it is a word which appears fairly frequently.
- When your child comes to an unfamiliar word, try saying one or two of the following:

  "Let's read the first bit again and then see if you can guess what it is."
  "Miss it out and read a bit more . . .now can you guess what it might say?"
  "Have a look at the beginning of the word, does that help?"
  "What would make sense there?"

  If your child *can't* guess the word in a matter of seconds, please *don't* prolong the agony – simply supply the word yourself.
- Whenever there has been any interruption to the reading as in the above, get your child to reread from the beginning of the sentence so that the flow of meaning is restored and she or he doesn't forget what they have just read.
- Praise all your child's attempts to work things out for him/herself. You don't have to go overboard – just acknowledge what has been done!
- No matter how hard it might be at times and no matter how justifiable a loss of patience might be, please don't become irritated with your child. You will never achieve anything like this except to raise your child's anxiety levels about reading which can have a damaging effect on progress.

- Do stop as soon as you feel your child is tiring or losing interest or you are becoming irritated because of what your child is doing or not doing. An enjoyable five minutes achieves a great deal more than ten minutes which are a struggle!
- Should your child bring home a book which is obviously too difficult (where there is more than one word in every ten which is not known, for example) do give her or him some support. You could try reading a few lines yourself and then have your child read them afterwards or you could try the paired reading technique which is explained after this section. If you do find that a reading book is too hard for your child then it is a sensible idea to have a quiet word with the teacher. She may suggest either a change of book or that you give your child more support such as I have outlined above. The important thing is that she knows about any difficulty that has been experienced at home.

The answers to two common worries

The problem of guessing Some parents worry that encouraging children to guess at unfamiliar words is encouraging them to take the easy way out. This really is not the case. As I explained in the section on how children learn to read, we do need to encourage children to use those three sources of clues and information to puzzle out what unfamiliar words might be (meaning, syntax – appreciation of the way words 'hang together', and the sound to symbol system of the language.) Working out an unfamiliar word needs to be a kind of problem-solving activity in which these clues are used. By asking children to guess a word we are helping them to do this; asking them to re-read or read on and use the beginning letters of the word gives them guidance in *how* to guess. What you can then do is help the child to check a guess by asking:

- Does it make sense? (meaning)
- Does it sound right? (syntax)
- Does what you've said match the look of the word? (sound-symbol awareness)

Guesses do need to be checked because it is no use allowing a child to develop the habit of saying the first thing which comes into his/her head and which bears no relation at all to what is on the page. If your child does this then you can encourage more productive guessing by asking the questions above.

The word-by-word reader Some children in the early stages of learning to read do so with a very plodding, word-by-word, expressionless voice. It is quite common and can be helped by asking the child either to read it again as if they were talking or to repeat what has been said by you, i.e. giving an example of how something might be said. This kind of reading behaviour can also be the result of trying to read material which is too difficult.

Paired reading

Paired reading is a technique which quite a few schools ask parents to carry out at home. Such schools would normally offer detailed guidance on how this should be done but, basically, it involves the following:

- The child chooses anything at all that he or she wants to read.
- Sitting side by side the parent and child real aloud together. Care has to be taken for the adult not to read too quickly and he or she should run a finger smoothly under the line of print as they read.
- Eventually, if the child wants to read alone, he/she gives a pre-arranged signal and the parent stops reading. The signal can be a nudge in the ribs or a tap

on the book – whatever has been decided before the reading starts.

- If the child runs into any difficulty at all (makes a mistake or meets an unfamiliar word) the parent waits three or four seconds and then corrects the mistake or supplies the unfamiliar word. The parent continues reading with the child until the child signals for the parent to stop.

The use of the paired reading technique is particularly useful with children who are having any problems with reading; it helps their confidence and allows them to read a range of material which would otherwise be too difficult so providing them with a lot of actual reading experience.

A final word. . .

As we all know, books are expensive items for schools to buy so it is a nice idea if you can provide a book bag for your child which will offer books some protection on the journeys to and from school. This can be a simple carrier bag, a plastic bag (longer lasting) or a specially made fabric bag which children can decorate themselves with fabric pens. Having a particular, easily identifiable book bag for school reading books does mean, as well, that it is easier for you and your child to find each morning in the rush to get to school on time! Reminding your child to take back school books the next morning can be a bind but is important. There is nothing more infuriating for teachers than to discover that the book they want to work on with the child is still at home. It's not much help to the child either!

THE QUESTIONS PARENTS ASK

How soon should I begin teaching my child to read?

Following the parents in the cartoons on the next page might be a little extreme! However, it is true to say that the earlier the start the better. This does *not* mean actually teaching your baby to read. What it does mean is this:

- The foundations of reading are to be found in talking because, as has been said already, it is through acquiring speech that the vast majority of children learn about language and its rules. It is *never* too soon to start talking to babies and the general rule for all pre-school children is: the more talk the better – take every possible opportunity to talk with your child. Talk about what you are doing at home and your surroundings when you go out, talk about what your child is doing when playing, in fact, talk about anything and everything you are doing together. That is the way your pre-school child will develop his or her language skills and learn new words and ideas.

- Introduce your child to books as soon as possible. At first these may simply be objects to play with or draw to your young child's attention – for example the plastic 'bath books' that you can buy. Because of the likelihood of the first books being playthings, they should obviously be sturdy – the books with pages made of thick card instead of paper, board books.
  As soon as your child begins to take any notice of the book itself (rather than just another object to play with) talk about the book. The time when your child begins to do this is the time to start reading stories or looking at picture books.

    The first stories read to children should be short and fairly simple. Don't

expect a child to listen to a whole story right from the start, stop the minute your child wants to. It is important that the first story reading sessions are enjoyable so, naturally, have your child on your lap as you read or talk about a book.

You will soon learn which are the stories your child enjoys because she or he will want them read again and again *and* again! When you are reading favourite stories run your finger under the lines as you read and, occasionally, say things like "These are the words which tell me what to say so that I can read it to you." Before too long, your child will know a story rather well and woe betide you if you miss out a bit or change things! This is the time when you can leave out words for your child to say. e.g. "Who's been eating *my* porridge said. . ." You may well find that your child is beginning to join in with you anyway – not because they are reading the words but because they know chunks off-by-heart.

- The child who is at this stage is the child who is ready to look at certain words and be told what they say. Never force this though, wait until your child shows an interest in this aspect. An interest in words and what they say can be fostered in many ways. We live in a print-filled environment and there are signs and labels all about us – it's by no means unusual to find that the first word a child can read is, for example *Esso*!
- Many pre-school children think that they can read and you may experience this with your own child when you see them sitting down with a favourite book. They will turn the pages and 'read' the story (perhaps to a toy or a pet) and it is not unknown for young children to announce that they can 'read this with my eyes shut'! The child, of course, is saying what has been learned by heart or describing what is in the pictures and if she or he thinks they can

read then that is fine at this stage and he/she should never have the truth pointed out.

- Learning books in this way does help children to begin to learn what certain words say and they will recognise them elsewhere. Some parents write labels to stick on objects in the home, for example: *door*, *television* or *This is Vicky's room*. If the labels are put up with Blu-tack then you can make a game of taking them down and putting them up again with your child's help. Never have too many labels up at once, however, four or five at a time is enough. (Apart from that, it doesn't exactly lead to domestic harmony if every time you go to pick something up a label falls off it!)
- Above all, never force the pace of your child's learning. If your child shows interest in something then do it, if not. . .don't! Pre-school children will let you know if they want to do something or not so let your child set his or her own pace.

Home schemes

Are reading schemes and materials for home use a good idea?

The short answer to this is: yes. . . and no.

They are *not* a good idea if they lead to any kind of pressure being put on a child to learn to read. Making a reluctant child work at home in order to accelerate progress is only likely to lead to rebellion at some later stage. They *are* a good idea if the materials are:

- bright and exciting;
- written by someone who really does know their business and who understands what is happening in schools;
- genuinely appealing to children;
- likely to provide you with some support in helping your child to learn.

The 'learning at home' published range of materials has expanded enormously in recent years as a result of increased awareness and demand. It is fair to say that much of what is available does indeed meet the points set out above, but there are some publications which really are not worth buying – their approach is very out of date. It would be impossible to give you an exhaustive list of what is available so instead I have chosen one major project as an example of what, in my view, is worth looking at. Do please remember, however, that there are other smaller series around which are very good.

Puddle Lane published by Ladybird is an extensive scheme with a fantasy, magical setting and the books are intended to be read by both the parent and the child. ITV do a Puddle Lane television programme and there is a range of materials available in addition to the books which includes cassette tapes of the stories. Although it is intended for home use, there are some infant schools who use the scheme as well – perhaps because it is written by a highly respected educational author, Sheila McCullagh.

These days you will find learning at home materials in newsagents, supermarkets and in a variety of shops –not to mention, of course, bookshops. In addition, there are bookclubs and mail-order services which are advertised, for example, in magazines. Such materials and books, then, are widely available but do, please, bear the following points in mind:

One afternoon, the Wideawake Mice were all fast asleep, in their home in Candletown Market.
The sun was shining down outside, and the mice were all very warm and comfortable.

A bee came buzzing in under the roof.
The bee buzzed in Miranda's ear.
Miranda woke up.
The bee flew off, into the sunshine.

Miranda woke up.

A Ladybird Puddle Lane book

Never buy a whole series before you are certain that your child will enjoy using it – unless, of course, there is some kind of 'money back' safeguard.

If at all possible, let your child have a look at whatever it is that you are considering buying – that will give you a much better idea of whether or not it is something which your child will *want* to use.

Never try to force your child into working at home with you.

Never put any pressure on your child to attempt things which are too difficult.

Children who work happily with enjoyment, who are working at their correct level, and therefore achieve success, are children who will make good progress with reading and writing and find them rewarding activities. Unless you are *sure* that your child really wants to work at home with you and the materials you have selected, it would be sensible to avoid buying home-learning schemes – at least for the time being. Stick to books!

The alphabet

When should I teach my child the alphabet?

Children are ready to learn the alphabet by heart when they have made a start on learning to read. As with most aspects of learning, there is a period of preparation or familiarisation which is necessary before any formal learning of the alphabet and you can certainly help with that from a pre-school stage. Two things are helpful: alphabet books and alphabet friezes.

Alphabet books Never buy an alphabet book without having a very careful read through of each page beforehand. There are some beautiful ABC books around which are a waste of time for most children because of the level of sophistication they demand. Look for the following:

- Are the animals, objects or whatever likely to mean something to your child or are they at least able to be explained fairly easily? "I is for Iguana" doesn't mean very much to the average four year old!
- Are the illustrations clear, bright and colourful? Are they in a fairly simple and easy to interpret style which will, because of the detail, provide lots to talk about and discuss?
- Most teachers would prefer ABC books to present children with the letter sounds which they are likely to learn first, for example:

  c:*cat*, *carrot* or *cot* rather than words like *circus* or *centipede*
  g:words like *girl*, *ghost* or *guitar* rather than *giant* or *gem*
  vowels: a as in *apple* rather than *ape*; e as in *egg* rather than *equal*; i as in *ink* rather than *ice*; o as in *orange* rather than *open*; u as in *umbrella* rather than *unicorn*.

- If it is to do its job properly, i.e. familiarise children with the alphabet, an ABC book needs to be read many times. You need, therefore, to choose one which your child will *want* to read many times. You will find some suggestions at the end of the book.

Alphabet friezes An alphabet frieze which a child can have in her/his own room is an excellent idea. You can:

- buy a published one;
- make one yourself, for example, pictures from magazines and photos. Include family photographs where possible e.g. m is for mummy, – is for child's name etc;
- use sheets of ABC wrapping paper. There are three or four of these now available which can be put up whole or cut into strips for a frieze.

Home-made friezes do have the advantage of being 'personal' to a child and it is

something which parent and child can make and build up together. It is a good idea to start with, say, A, B and C and then gradually add more letters. Read the frieze to and with your child, saying, for example: "A is for apple, B is for Barry, C is for cake. . .A,B,C!" pointing as you read. You can then extend this idea by making an ABC scrapbook with lots of pictures which are labelled for each letter. This has the advantage of showing the child that *lots* of words begin with certain letters and not just one!

Letter sounds

How can I help my child to learn the letter sounds?

Letter sounds are important as I've said earlier because children who know their letter sounds can look at the beginning of an unfamiliar word and then make an informed guess as to what the word might be, using the context or meaning of the rest of the sentence and the sound at the beginning of the word.

To begin with, let's remind ourselves of what sound for each letter needs to be taught first. Some letters do, of course,

have more than one sound but it's best to stick to what the teacher is likely to be doing in school. The sounds you should use are:

a as in apple
b as in bear
c as in cat
d as in dog
e as in egg
f as in fish
g as in garden
h as in house
i as in insect
j as in jump
k as in king
l as in little
m as in monkey
n as in nail
o as in octopus
p as in penny
q as in queen
r as in rabbit
s as in sun
t as in table
u as in umbrella
v as in van
w as in wind
x as in fox
y as in yellow
z as in zoo

It's actually very hard to say these sounds in isolation without adding an extra 'r' or 'uh' sound *but you do need to try and avoid doing this*. The MMMmmm sound is made, for example, by keeping your lips pressed together. It's always best to avoid giving children the idea that letters *always* make certain sounds by saying, for example, ''this letter usually says. . .'' rather than ''this letter says. . .''

Here are some suggestions as to how you can help your child learn the sounds:

Use alphabet books and friezes as in the answer to the previous question.
When your child is reading to you and comes to an unfamiliar word, point to the first letter and say the sound. Where words begin with more than one consonant, then give the sounds together e.g. *string. . .str; flower. . .fl; swan. . .sw; scrape. . .scr; spade. . .sp; shop. . .sh; chin. . .ch*
Very simple tongue twisters can be fun too. For example:

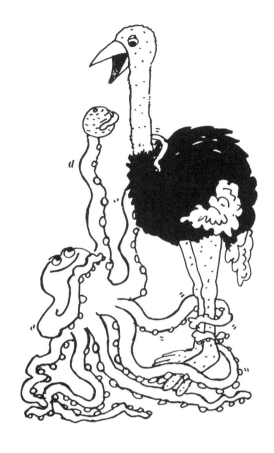

Polly picked the peaches and pears.
The wicked witches wore wellies on
    Wednesdays.
Michael's mum makes marvellous
    marmalade.
Tony's tomatoes tasted terrible.
Baby bear bounces the ball.
Five funny fish made five funny faces.
Hairy Harry had a horrible hat.
Naughty Nellie nipped Nana's nose.
The red rabbit likes radishes and rhubarb.
Gertie the goat gobbled gloves in the
    garden.
Dino's dopey dog dances in his dinner.
Carol carries her cat curled in her coat.
Ann dropped an apple on the astronaut's
    ankle.
Johnny Juggler jumped in the jelly.
Incey the insect is in the ink.
Vera's violet vest is by Victor's violin.
The end of Emma's empty egg is on the
    edge of the plate.
Sarah sits on the sand in the sun.
Luke likes lollipops less than lemonade.

The octopus offered the ostrich an
    orange for its tea.
I like yellow yachts, yo-yos and yoghurt.
Zebedee the zebra went zipping through
    the zoo.
Uncle's umbrella is upstairs under the
    bed.
Max fixed the box for the six foxes.
The queen asked the question quietly.
Cook a kipper in a kettle and keep it for a
    king.

4 I Spy is an excellent game for helping children to learn their letter sounds. Play it by giving the *sound* of the letter rather than the name e.g. *ssss* instead of 'ess'.

Do remember, however, children should not be expected to begin learning sounds until they are capable of reading early, simple stories for themselves; in other words, making a start on reading must precede learning letter sounds – not the other way round. Neither should children be expected to learn a lot of letters all at once. It is better to start with two or three which appear at the beginning of words the child already knows (his or her own name, for example) and then introduce a couple more when the first ones are known. The other point to bear in mind is that you should avoid teaching together any letters which have similar sounds (m and n, b and p, d and t, for example.) Choosing letters with contrasting sounds e.g. m and t or s, w and d, is likely to make the learning easier and avoid unnecessary confusions.

Dislike of school reading scheme

My child hates his school reading scheme. . . what can I do about it?

The first thing to do is to try and be sure *why* he hates it. Is it because he is reading books which are too difficult for him and so he gets frustrated and disheartened? Does he not like the characters in the stories) Does he not like the stories (or lack of stories; in any, all or some of the books? Do try and talk to him about it because you also need to be sure that it is a genuine aversion to the scheme itself and not towards reading in general or reading to you at home specifically.

The next thing to do is to make arrangements to see his class teacher. The best way of tackling this is to write a note asking if you could go and talk about your child's reading on such and such a date or an alternative one if that is not convenient.

When you do talk to the teacher, don't be surprised if she or he is not aware of your child's feelings – children can often disguise the way they feel about something in front of teachers. Tell the teacher everything and do point out that you are concerned that your child is in serious danger of being put off reading altogether.

The teacher will then, in all probability, do one of the following things:

- try a different scheme or series of books with your child – perhaps on a temporary basis;
- change books within the scheme if the major problem seems to be that the current reading material is either too difficult or too easy;
- be very apologetic and explain that she has no alternative (for a variety of possible reasons) except to keep your child on the scheme.

Where does that leave you? Well, the first two options should solve the problem. The third is more difficult. The most likely reasons for not doing anything about it are either lack of alternative books in school or using the reading scheme as a focus for much of the reading and language work in class, which means that the children need to read the books.

Under such circumstances the best you can do as a parent is:

1 Talk to your child and explain that you understand the problem but that he will have to continue using the books for the time being. If he dislikes the scheme because he thinks the stories and characters are silly you might like to follow what someone I know did. Their reading at home sessions of the scheme which her son loathed was greatly enlivened when he was permitted first of all to invent silly voices for the silly characters and then to invent alternative stories. That way a 'necessary evil' became not only tolerable but some fun too.

2 Do your utmost to encourage your child to read other books as well and make sure that you do provide books by, for

example, regular visits to the public library. The reading aloud by you of stories which are too difficult for your child to read alone is also important. Your child will then be getting three lots of reading experience: the reading scheme, the books you provide at his reading level and the books and stories you read aloud. This may sound a lot but it is important to ensure that he has lots of enjoyable reading experiences to offset the less satisfactory one.

There is, of course, the possibility that your child's school is using a very outdated reading scheme and that he is by no means the only one who is not enjoying it. If you know this to be the case and there are several parents who are concerned, then the best thing is to talk to the headteacher about it. Perhaps you could ask if it would be possible to arrange a 'curriculum' evening for parents when the question of reading in the school could be discussed and explained.

Talking about stories

My child's teacher is always telling parents to talk about the story when we are reading with our children. What exactly does this mean?

The point of talking about what children are reading is to help them think about what they are reading, to interpret and understand it. It is also a means of helping them to develop their language skills, enhance their enjoyment of a story and, of course, a way of checking on their understanding. When a child is talking about what they have read you can soon tell if they've got the wrong end of the stick about something!

Talking about a story also means talking about the illustrations. We 'read' pictures just as much as we read words and not only do illustrations add something to a story but they can also tell part of a story. Information is often conveyed in pictorial or

diagramatic form so it is obviously important to be able to understand pictures and to attend to the details in them. While it is natural to make comments about a picture such as "That's a scary looking witch isn't it?" or simply "That's nice!" we do need to try and do something more sometimes. Questions and comments such as the following can help towards getting children to really think about illustrations.

"I wonder what that is supposed to be?" (pointing to some detail)

"Why do you think the giant is looking like that?"

"I like the look of what's happening here!"

"I like this bit of the picture best, which do you like?"

"What's your favourite picture that we've looked at?. . . Why do you like that one?"

"Can you guess from the picture what you think is going to happen in this part of the story? Let's both guess and then we'll read it and see who was right".

When it comes to talking about the story there are questions you can ask during the reading and questions to ask afterwards. For example, you could choose from:

During the reading:
"Can you guess what she's going to do next?"

"I think so and so is going to (make a wrong/silly prediction). What do you think?"

"Can you guess what's going to happen in the next part of the story?"

"Now I wonder why he/she did/said that?"

"Ooh, do you think that was a nice thing to do?"

"Can you remember why she did that?"

"I don't understand this. . .what did he do that for?"

After the reading:
"Did you enjoy that?. . .Why?"

"What was your favourite bit of the story?"

"Were there any bits that you didn't like?"

"I can't remember, why did so and so do such and such?"

"Do you think the story could have had a different ending?"

"Who did you like best in the story?"

"Choose your favourite bit of the story and we'll go and read it to mummy. You'll have to tell her what the story is about though or she won't know what's going on."

All these are fairly general questions and comments which could apply to most of the things your child is reading – obviously there will be particular details and happenings in individual books that you might want to pick up on or check. Don't go overboard on asking questions each time your child reads or listens to a story though, will you? The last thing you want to do is to spoil the pleasure of the story!

Reading choice

Should I read anything other than stories to my child?

YES! Read poems, rhymes, jokes and information books – anything at all that you think your child will be interested in. This includes things like snippets from the newspaper, magazines and Radio/T.V. Times. Not only are you helping to extend your child's general experience and knowledge but you are also introducing her or him to a range of different types of text and enabling your child to listen to language being used in different ways.

Reading to my child

My child is reading quite well now so should I stop reading to her?

My advice to parents is always to go on reading aloud for as long as your child wants to listen to you and don't stop simply because you feel she ought to be able to

read for herself now. The majority of children like to be read to right the way through primary school and there are always books which children would enjoy but which might be too long or complicated for them to read by themselves.

Many nine or ten year old children, for example, would love the timeless classic *Black Beauty* but may not yet be ready to tackle the book by themselves. Reading a chapter at a time aloud each evening can be both an enjoyable and moving experience for parent and child alike (the book has it's sad moments too as it gives us an insight into times gone by.)

All of us, children and adults alike, can learn so much from books. They open up our imaginations, take us on journeys we could never otherwise make – journeys to different times and different places, they give us the chance to touch good and to touch evil from the safety and security of our own homes, they are a means of extending our experience and knowledge of the world and of humanity.

Television

Is it true that if children watch too much television their reading will suffer?

It's too easy to turn television into some kind of malignant monster which gobbles up our time and destroys the quality of our

lives. Television can broaden horizons as well and there are avid viewers who are also avid readers (I speak as one who is both!)

I think it is the quality of the television experience which matters as much as the quantity. Sensible parents always have and always will censor their children's viewing, discuss what they have seen and not allow their sensitivities to become blunted through crass and thoughtless over-exposure to, for example, the violent. It is a shame if children are permitted to sit passively in front of the television for hours on end every evening. I personally would ration television for children to an hour or two each day (depending of course on their bedtime) so that there is time to talk, to play and to read – and do homework later on.

Whether or not children get into the reading habit will depend on their parents *making time* for reading and encouraging children to share and listen to stories. If in order to do that you have to turn off the television, then so be it!

Encourage writing

What should I be doing to encourage my young child where writing is concerned?

To get young children interested in reading, we read to them and give them books from an early age. It's a very similar thing with writing.

Just as you want to make sure that your

child sees *you* reading at home, make sure that you also write in front of children too. Tell them what you are doing, for example:

"We need some more milk today, let's write a note to the milkman and ask him to leave some, shall we? I'll need a pencil and a bit of paper first. . . .Now then, what shall I write? I'll write 'Please leave three pints of milk today. Thank you.' Do you want to read it with me?"

Follow the same approach when you write a letter, a message, a shopping list or whatever – not *every* time you write something unless you've got heaps of time to spare, but perhaps once a week or so.

Writing a letter to someone your child Knows as well can provide the opportunity to let your child have a go, too:

"I'm writing a letter to granny to tell her how we're getting on. Would you like to write to her as well?'

Given paper and pencil or crayons your child will probably scribble. That's good. Ask him or her to tell you what the letter says (so that you add a translation in your own letter if you want!) and let your child put the letter in the envelope with your own.

It's a sure thing that once your child has discovered the joys of making marks on

paper you'll want to keep an eye on the walls and other property! Some parents find that to have a large bit of paper fixed at child height on which the child *is* allowed to scribble can help overcome this problem. It also makes sense to keep odd bits of paper in a certain place so that children can help themselves when they want to write and draw. Do show your child how much you value his or her attempts by putting them on a special place on the wall.

Being given the opportunity to scribble etc. is how a child learns to control a pencil or crayon. Soon, you are likely to see your child trying out what they have learned from watching you writing – scribbling in lines and making shapes which look something like letters. This is the time when you can begin to teach your son or daughter how to write his or her name. You can do it by:

- writing the name as the child watches, in letters about two and a half cms. (one inch) high;
- holding and guiding his/her hand to make the letters;
- getting her or him to write on top of your writing i.e. the child copying the letters;
- making letters out of plasticene or play dough and letting your child feel the shapes and run a finger over them guided by you so that the correct direction is followed.

Gradually your child will master this and show an interest in writing other things, which is perhaps the best way of teaching her or him to write all the letters.

In all of this don't forget the golden rules. . .

- do it only if your child shows interest in writing;
- make sure you praise and value all your child's attempts;
- help your child to learn the correct formation of the letters right from the start;

- share your own writing activities with your child – that is the way that children learn about the purposes of writing;
- keep some of your child's early attempts at writing – they will be fun to look back at in years to come and something to treasure.

It is important to value the writing that children do, not just in the early stages but later on when they are writing at school as well as at home. So do set aside a special place in your home where you can display your child's work which is brought home.

Reading games

Are there any games I could play with my child to help her reading?

Games are a good way of getting children to learn something; they learn almost in spite of themselves because it is the game itself which is the important thing as far as they are concerned. Some parents say that they never know quite how to introduce a game so that their child will want to play it. Personally, I think the straight-forward approach usually works: "I know a good game that we haven't played before, shall we play it now?"

Games you can adapt

Snakes and Ladders for the older child can easily be adapted to make a reading game. All you need is fifteen to twenty pieces of card on which you have written whatever it is that you want your child to read. This could be single words, sentences, questions e.g. "What is your name?" "Where do you live?" "How old are you?" "What colour is your hair?" (There are lots of high frequency words in questions like that!) Instead of using dice to play the game, you take it in turns to read a card aloud, answer the question if there is one and then count the number of words on the card

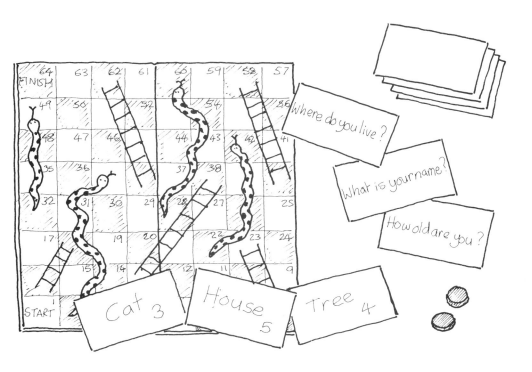

That is the number of spaces you move on the board. If you are using single words, however, then write a number on each card to indicate the number of moves to make.

Scrabble is too hard for young children but if you have a set at home you can use the individual letters to play with. For example: make up a word, tell your child what it is and then ask her to find the letters to copy it. At a slightly more advanced stage use the letters for learning about alphabetical order or make up a word, read it and then take a letter away while your child shuts her eyes. She then has to find the letter from within a group of six or so. *Scrabble* letters can also be used to make one word into another. For example: Use the following letters: a, y, m, s, p, l, d, h, r and w. Make the word *play* and show your daughter how you can make new words by: taking away

the p to make *lay*, taking away the l and putting back the p to make *pay*. Let your child have a go at doing the same thing and then take it in turns to make new words with the other letters. This can be quite difficult for some children so do make sure you read the words each time – the whole word, not sounding it out.

You can easily use small pieces of card on which you have written the letters instead of Scrabble tiles. Do bear in mind that Scrabble titles show the capital form of the letters which your child may not be used to yet.

Games you can make up

Snap You can play snap with pictures and words. On half the cards write words and on the other half draw a picture of each word (or use pictures cut from magazines and stuck on). If the words are all new to your child, then spend time going through them and letting her match the pictures with the words. Don't use words which are visually very similar and don't introduce too many new words at once – three or four at a time is plenty.

Hunt the thimble/penny/whatever Prepare some cards on which you write: 'under the table', 'on the table', 'next to the television', 'behind the chair', 'under the chair', 'on the chair', 'next to the window', 'behind the door'. Read the cards with your child. Then take it in turns to hide the thimble in one of the places on the cards. The other person holds up a card for a yes or no answer and, depending on the answer, goes to look for the thimble. You will naturally have to help out with the reading to begin with.

Collecting words Make lots of word cards which you can put on or by objects in the room: television, table, chair, carpet, door, window, and so on. You can then:

- ask your child to collect all the ones beginning with a certain letter;
- collect the right card in response to a clue e.g. you sit on this;
- muddle all the cards up and get her to put them back in their right places;
- take a couple away and see if she can spot which ones are missing;
- ask her to read them – first of all in their places and then when she has collected them up.

Story people Your child is bound to have favourite stories and favourite characters which you will know as well. You can:

- describe a story person and get her to guess who you are talking about;
- get her to do the same for you;

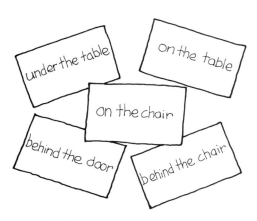

Make the cards a reasonable size – about 3" × 12" or 7cm × 30cm.

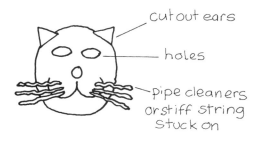

- use the pictures in a book to help you make a mask of the character – a simple oval shape which a child holds in front of the face is easiest and safest.

This last one isn't a reading game – it's simply lots of fun!

Nursery rhymes

Are nursery rhymes important in this day and age and, if so, why?

Nursery rhymes are a part of our literary heritage and history and they have been enjoyed by countless thousands of children over the years. Most of the rhymes we still enjoy have their roots in a long forgotten historical event – it is the rhyme we remember not its origins, although this can be a fascinating study for adults. Did you know, for example, that the famous *Ring-a-ring o'roses, a pocket full of posies* goes back to the time of the plague and refers to the red blotches and sneezes which were part of the symptoms?

Nursery rhymes have a rhythm and flow to the language which makes them fascinating as well as having appealing characters like Humpty Dumpty. Rhymes

like this can have another function too; they can be a thoroughly enjoyable way to introduce children to rhyme. An appreciation of rhyme is important; it is one of the ways in which children learn about the patterns of words. This is helpful for spelling as well as reading. The child who understands about the common pattern of letters in, for example: *play, stay, may* and *say* is the child who is able to have a very good go at spelling *away*.

So, yes, nursery rhymes are important and well worth reading to your child!

Books at the right level

When I go to the library or bookshop how can I be sure that I am getting a book which is at the right level for my child?

This *is* tricky to be sure about! Many books with just a small amount of text on the page can, in fact, be quite difficult for a child to read because of the language and words which are used. Some books with a lot of text can be much easier to read than you might think. So it is not a good idea to think of the difficulty level of the book solely in terms of how much print there is on the page.

The best way of checking whether or not a particular book is right for your child is to be guided by her. Encouraging her to choose her own books is far more likely to result in her ending up with a book that she really wants to read. If she chooses one which is too hard you can support her reading by sharing the reading in the ways explained earlier in the book or by reading it to her to begin with. If she chooses one which is easy to read, it doesn't matter – she *has* chosen it so *wants* to read it and even an 'easy' read is a good read because it is providing her with an opportunity to practise and consolidate her developing skills.

There is a method of checking the

difficulty level of a book which some parents find helpful called the 'Five Finger Test'. It will provide a *very* rough guide as to whether or not a particular book is at an appropriate level and this is what you do:

- ask your child to read the first page of the book to herself;
- if she comes to a word that she doesn't know, she puts a finger on it;
- if she runs out of fingers (of one hand) before she gets to the end of the page then the book is probably too difficult for her to read alone.

This is based on the expectation that many children's books have 50–100 words on the page and, in anything which is to be read independently, there should be no more than about one in every twenty words which are unfamiliar to the child.

Reading scheme books at home

My local bookshop stocks the reading scheme my children use. Is it a good idea for me to buy the books to help them get on?

There is only one set of circumstances where I would suggest that a parent does this and that is where a child has enjoyed a particular book so much that she or he would dearly like to have a copy of their own to reread to their hearts content. Otherwise, I would say no. I say this for the following reasons:

1 You may, unwittingly, give the children 'the next book' before they are ready for it.

48

2 The teacher is probably using the books in conjunction with other materials e.g. published workbooks/worksheets or apparatus which the school have devised especially. In order for this work to be most effective, the teacher needs to keep the reading of the books in step with other activities. This cannot be done if parents are supplying children with additional books from the scheme.

3 All children need to read books other than those from the reading scheme – no matter how good it is – both in order to build a broad and solid foundation for their developing skills and to extend their experience of books in general. Money for books is, therefore, better spent on different books. Your children's teachers should be able to make some suggestions of books which would be good choices if you are at a loss as to what books to get (and they will probably be delighted that you approach it in this way.)

Help with spelling

My child's reading is coming along nicely but his spelling is not very good at all – what can I do to help?

It is quite common for children's reading to be better than their spelling but it is a mistake to think that by reading more and more a child's spelling will automatically improve – it won't. Some children seem to develop spelling ability very easily but the vast majority need a lot of help and teaching. All children need to be taught a way of learning to spell both new words and those which cause them problems.

Left to their own devices, children will often try to learn a word by repeating the letter names over and over to themselves. This may be a way of remembering something for the short term, but it is not likely to result in long term learning. The best way of illustrating this is to think about

what happens when you need to look up a telephone number. You look it up, repeat the number two or three times and then dial it. You can remember which number to dial then, but if you were asked what that number is a few hours later you wouldn't be able to recall it.

The method which is in very successful use in many schools is to teach children to learn words by the *Look, Cover, Write, Check* routine which is as follows.

1 The word needing to be learned is written down correctly for or by the child on a piece of paper or in a special spelling notebook.
2 The child goes through the following steps – with any help which may be required:

LOOK

Look   at the word very carefully paying special attention to any tricky parts (e.g. the *au* pattern in *because*). Say the word out loud and if pronouncing it in a funny way by sounding letters which are really silent will help, then do it (e.g. saying *Wednesday* as Wed-nes-day.)

COVER

Cover   the word up – either with a finger or a piece of paper/card.

WRITE

Write   the word from memory

CHECK

Check   back with the original word to see if the attempt has been successful or which part of the word has been incorrectly spelled.

REPEAT

Repeat   the steps until the child is able to write the word (from memory each time) easily and fluently.

You may wonder why copying out a word several times won't do instead. The reason for this not being very effective is that when children copy something it is almost as if they go on to automatic pilot – they can copy correctly without paying full attention to what they are doing. Writing a word from memory means that their brains have to be fully engaged!

If your child has not been taught this method at school then do teach it to him yourself and encourage him to use it. Children *do* need reminding about this because it is obviously harder work than simply copying something!

When he is writing and asks you how to spell something, then this is what you can do:

1 Always write the word down for him – don't just say the letter names.
2 Let him simply copy the word into his writing at this stage so that he doesn't loose the flow of the writing or his train of thought.
3 When the writing is finished, go back to the words that he asked you how to spell and select three or four for him to learn

using the method above. Choose the words which are ones that appear frequently in writing; it is more important for him to be able to spell words like *because*, *very*, *where*, *was* or *have* than it is to spell words like *dinosaur*, *Transformers* or *galactic* at this stage!

4 You may also want to help by looking at the finished piece of writing with him. Try doing it like this:

- Ask him to read what he has written.
- Praise the content and tell him which bits you like particularly.
- Ask him if there are any words which he thinks he has spelled wrongly.
- Discuss these words with him and perhaps draw his attention to a few mispellings if he hasn't been able to identify any of his own mistakes.
- Don't forget to praise him for making an attempt to spell the words himself.
- Select two or three of the words for him to learn.

Do please remember that if he has made a lot of mistakes in his writing you should NOT point them *all* out. Doing this is only likely to result in making him feel overwhelmed and disheartened and so more reluctant to write anything in the future.

If you are going to go through your child's writing with him in this way then it makes obvious sense to do it immediately he has finished and leave step number three until last.

It is a very good idea to have a separate notebook for spelling at home rather than you writing and your child learning words on pieces of paper. That way you keep a record of the words he has been learning or needs to learn which can be checked from time to time.

Another technique which may be handy for your child to use is one which teachers and children have christened 'The Magic Line'. When a child wants to write a word which she or he cannot spell they do as much as they can of the word and then draw a line for the rest. For example, let's take the word *because*: one child might write be_____, another might put b_____ or bec_____ while the child who hasn't got a clue will simply put _____. When they have finished their writing they go through and fill in the missing letters with the teacher's help – or in your child's case, your help.

Children with spelling difficulties or those who are still in the process of learning how to spell need to have their attention drawn to the structure and common patterns of words. You might like to try some of the following ideas:

- Many children have problems with the words *when* and *what*. Point out that "There is a hen in when" or "a hat in what".
- Show your son links with other words; for example, if he can spell *her* then the following words are easy: *her, here, there, where*
- Make up silly sentences together which contain words with common letters. (It doesn't matter how the words are pronounced as long as they have the same pattern in them.) For example:

That's *done* it, the dog has *gone* and buried my *one* bone!
Move over, love, you're on my *glove!*
He c*augh*t his n*augh*ty d*augh*ter playing dr*augh*ts and l*augh*ing.
Did you *hear*, that *dear* little b*ear* w*ears* a p*ear* on his *ear*?!

Get your child to write out the sentences and draw pictures to go with them if he wants to.

Dictionaries

Is it a good idea to buy children a dictionary for use at home?

Yes, dictionaries can be fascinating things just to browse through and there are some lovely picture dictionaries available for younger children. Do please bear in mind however that dictionaries are not very easy things to use as far as children are concerned. They have to know about alphabetical order, how a word begins and have a rough idea of how a word is spelt in order for them to find a word – whether it is to check on the spelling or the meaning.

Unless your child is a *very* good reader and a *very* good speller, don't expect her or him to be able to use a dictionary without help. You will have to show them what to do in the first place and then continue to give them a lot of support for a long while. It is worth it though in order to get into the habit of checking in a dictionary. I know I couldn't manage without mine!

Help with handwriting

I'm very worried about my child's handwriting. Can I do anything to help improve it?

There are various aspects to handwriting which need to be considered when we think of improving it. This question usually arises in the mid-junior years so that is the stage of development that I shall concentrate on, listing each point and the things to look out for.

Right or left-handed? Left-handed children need extra guidance as to how to hold the pencil or pen – see page 23 for which grip to encourage. They also need to be shown how to position the paper or book they are writing on. Tilting the paper down to the right at an angle of about 45 degrees is probably most comfortable and stops the hand bending awkwardly:

When it comes to using a pen there are several alternatives. It is possible to buy fountain pens with a left handed nib – the ordinary ones are hopeless for left-handed people. Most children these days prefer to

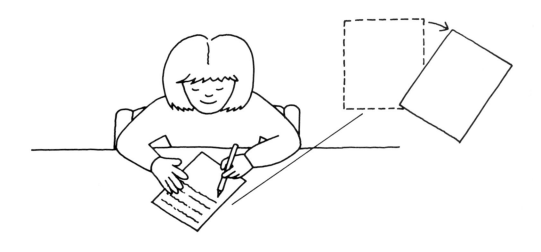

How to position writing paper for left-handed children

write with a roller ball or fibre-tipped pen and these do look better than biros very often. I would always suggest a fibre-tipped pen in preference to a fountain pen for left-handed children in particular. They are not prone to splodges and smudges to anything like the same degree. When children begin using ink as opposed to pencil you will often notice some deterioration in the handwriting as they get used to using a pen. This shouldn't last long, however, and should be only a temporary setback.

Pencil grip Do check how your child is holding the pencil and encourage a grip which is both comfortable and allows proper control of the pencil. (See page 23.) Some children press very hard when they write which is tiring and hard work, resulting sometimes in handwriting which deteriorates as more is written. They need to be encouraged to relax their grip more.

Holding the paper This may seem silly but there *are* children who don't keep the paper

or book in place with the non-writing hand with the obvious result that the paper or book moves and the child's writing suffers each time.

Letter formation Forming the individual letters correctly is crucial to good handwriting so check to see if this is the problem with your child. The best way is to ask her or him to copy out a sentence which contains all the letters of the alphabet while you watch closely. Here are two example sentences to choose from:

The quick brown fox jumps over the lazy dog.
The six jet planes zoomed quickly over the big flight tower.

(Incidentally, getting your child to make up his or her own alphabet sentences can provide good handwriting practice!)
    If you look back to page ?, you will see how each letter should be formed and so will be able to help your child correct any that are not right. It is worth mentioning

that one of the biggest problems in learning a joined style of writing can be where children form their letters in an unorthodox way – even though the finished product looks alright in the printed form.

Spacing between words Children will often leave too little or too much space between words which makes the writing more difficult to read. Leaving a space about the size of the letter m is a pretty good guide to spacing – an m in the child's writing, not this print, by the way!

Overall size of writing Although it is difficult to be precise about this all adults will recognise writing that is too small and cramped or writing that is overlarge! Writing that fills the space between two lines is too large, for example.

Letter size and position on the line In handwriting the letters should be of an even height as in:

man   hklbd

except for t which is shorter than bdlk and h. They should also be correctly positioned in relation to the line:

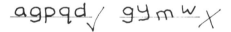

If this is a problem with your child's writing, then it may help him or her to see what is wrong if you draw a straight line across the top of the writing to demonstrate where the letters should be as in:

Candy

Other points to look out for Bearing in mind the style of handwriting taught by the school, are the letters joined correctly? If

the actual letter formation is correct then this should be easy. The join is made simply by continuing on from the finishing point of one letter to the starting point of another. In some styles, however, not all letters *are* joined – b for example. This is why you need to be sure what style is in use in school.

Are the letters which are closed (e.g. o a b d) closed properly without gaps?

Is any slope to the letters regular? That is, letters do not slope in different directions e.g. a backward leaning b and a forward leaning d.

If your child gets 'b' the wrong way round, show him/her that it faces the same way as a capital b. You can demonstrate by making a small 'b' into a capital.

b   B   B

Practice Improving handwriting is never easy: it takes lots of practice which can be boring for children unless they are copying out something for a reason such as a letter to granny or a favourite poem to put up on your wall, for example. It's even more difficult if you are the one who thinks the handwriting needs improving and not your child. If you are in the fortunate position of having a child who is just learning to write, you can do a lot to prevent handwriting problems arising and bad habits being practised by making sure that your child learns to form letters correctly right from the start.

Some parents have found that all the above points to look for in handwriting have helped them to improve their own!

The school's role

Isn't it the school's job to teach my child to read and write?

Schools are there for the purpose of educating our children and, as learning to

read and write is a crucial part of that, then of course it is the school's job to teach them. It's also the school's job to look after and develop the physical and moral welfare of their pupils. But no-one expects them to do that single-handedly without parents playing an equally important part. It should be the same with reading and writing.

Someone once said that education is too important to be left to schools! I certainly don't believe that but I do believe that it shouldn't be left *only* to the schools. Think about the colossal amount of learning your child did or is doing during the period from birth until going to school. Who was the most crucial factor in all of that learning? You, the parents. Think of the number of hours your child spends in school and the number of hours that are spent at home. Do you think that learning stops at the school gates? Of course not!

You have a huge advantage over any teacher in school. You know your child better than a teacher ever can and you are hardly likely to have a family the size of the average class! You can add a very special something to your child's experience of learning to read and write; you can help her or him learn within that very special parent and child relationship. Your child is one of the handful of people that you care most about in the whole world – that cannot be true of a teacher and pupil relationship, no matter how good it is.

Comics

Will reading comics discourage my child from reading books?

This is highly unlikely. All children enjoy reading comics but as long as they have access to enjoyable books too, there shouldn't be a problem. Some comics are great and some are rubbish but you might like to think about the following point: How will children learn to recognise and then discard rubbish if they haven't read any in the first place?

Parents' reading

How important is this idea of letting your children see you reading?

Very! Children want to copy the behaviour of the people they admire so when your children see you reading you are providing them with a model. In addition, how can you expect your child to believe you when you tell them that reading is important if, as far as they know, it is something which you never do yourself?!

Which books?

What kind of books should my child be reading?

It depends on what kind of child you've got! Children, like anyone else, have different tastes in books – some prefer the humorous, some prefer information books, ten year olds tend not to like fairy stories much, six year olds do. One of the best sources of information for parents about children's books is the *Good Book Guide to Children's Books* published each year by Penguin Books. It is an extremely useful purchase which gives details and descriptions of a whole range of books in different categories and age ranges.

Not interested in books

My four year old son is not interested in books at all. What can I do?

Give him time. He could well be a very active child who is as yet unable to sit still for very long – this is often the case with pre-school children who are not interested in books. Don't worry. He's busy learning other things at this stage. Do keep on trying though; for such children bedtime is often

the time to catch them when they are feeling tired, less active and more prepared to listen for a short while. Try him with very short stories with lots of exciting pictures.

My 6/7/8 year old is not interested in reading, what can I do?

A list of things for you to check or try:

- Does your child have access to bright, colourful, interesting books at home which are on the easy rather than the difficult side?
- Have you tried enlisting the help of your nearest children's librarian? She or he should be able to recommend some books to borrow which are usually popular with your child's age and sex group.
- Have you tried taking your child to a bookshop and letting him or her browse and choose something which appeals? Do allow plenty of time for this and don't be afraid to explain what you are doing to the person in the shop – you are quite likely to get some good support and guidance for your child in that way.
- Are you still reading aloud to your child? It's one of the best ways of getting children hooked on books. Do vary the reading aloud matter so that you are trying all the categories which may appeal for example: adventure stories, animal stories, sci-fi, joke books, funny poems (try Roger McGough, Spike Milligan or Shel Silverstein, for example). It's a rare child who doesn't like Roald Dahl books in the mid to upper junior years so they are always worth trying. Is your child one who prefers information books to stories? Have a hunt through, for example, the Usborne paperback range – they do some really fascinating titles which your child might enjoy. They are also liberally illustrated.
- I take it the problem is one of can-read-but-doesn't rather than a reading

difficulty as such? Do check though because, for example, if a child has a history of struggling with print it is quite likely that he or she is not going to be very keen on the whole process. It is important that children in this category *and* those who are simply reluctant are given short, well-illustrated and fairly easy books to begin with. If those are accepted then you can introduce longer books – perhaps by reading the first part aloud and then sharing or taking turns at the reading, building up to letting your child finish off the book alone.

- You will not achieve anything by forcing your child to read or nagging – it simply doesn't work. If it *has* been an emotional bone of contention to date, drop it for a few weeks at least and don't say anything more about it. Try leaving the odd book around the place (without referring to it) or sitting and chuckling loudly over a book of jokes in your child's presence. Curiosity will

often work wonders in situations like this.

- There are an increasing number of children's books available on tape these days and some attractive book plus tape packages can be found in high street stores. These do have very widespread appeal but it is obviously worth sounding your child out about whether or not she/he thinks they *would* listen to one before you purchase.
- Do remember, as has been said elsewhere, seeing the rest of the family reading for pleasure *is* important. Some families have found that the introduction of a fifteen minute reading time where *everyone* in the family reads and then perhaps talks briefly about what has been read is a very pleasurable and relaxing experience for all. It can also make a significant change of attitude come about on the part of the reluctant reader.

READING DIFFICULTIES

Many parents ask advice concerning a child with reading difficulties. It does seem to be the case that more boys than girls have problems with reading but this section of the book is for parents of children of *either* sex who are having difficulty in learning to read.

What causes reading difficulties?

There are a large number of reasons why some children have problems with reading and, in all honesty, it is not always possible to be absolutely certain as to any one cause or combination of causes. It is unlikely that a single root of the problem can be identified with any degree of certainty. It is also true to say that for every child who has a particular problem or set of circumstances which are thought to be responsible for the reading difficulty, there will be another child with the same problems who learns to read with no trouble. For example, there are children of very low intelligence who don't learn to read and there are those of equally low intelligence who do. There are children who are profoundly deaf who learn to read well and others, equally deaf, who do not. That said, there are numerous reasons put forward for reading failure or for children experiencing difficulty with reading, some of which are:

- missing out on large chunks of schooling e.g. because of ill health;
- emotional disturbance or trauma at a crucial learning stage;
- sensory problems – vision or hearing loss;
- behaviour problems to the degree where a child is described as maladjusted;
- undue anxiety or pressure from parents;
- poor teaching at school or lack of continuing of teaching;
- inappropriate books and materials;
- dyslexia.

The effects of reading difficulties

The child is going to have problems with the written word but there are other possible difficulties as well – largely to do with self-image. It is very common for children who have reading difficulties to believe that they are having the problems because they are stupid. This, of course is not true but the child's perception of his or her abilities can become so fixed that it affects self-confidence and motivation towards other things as well. A child can give up trying to do anything at school because, believing himself to be stupid he 'knows' he will fail and so there isn't much point in doing anything. This kind of child may appear on the surface not to be bothered about the problem but this is rarely so – he is simply trying to protect the tattered remnants of his self-esteem by not attempting anything where he sees he is going to fail.

Other children react to their difficulties by becoming more and more anxious. Sometimes the anxiety is confined to the reading but quite often it will spill over into other aspects of their lives. Children have been known to worry that their parents won't love them if they don't learn to read. We know that is quite ridiculous but to a child it might be a very real fear. What often happens is the anxious child gets so 'uptight' about the whole thing that the anxiety itself can then block the learning.

What I have described are almost extremes of reactions to failure but it is true to say that with only a very few exceptions all children are worried by any difficulty with learning to read. What can you do about these side effects?

- Never let your own anxiety about your child's difficulties become apparent to him or her.
- Never discuss the problem with someone else in front of the child.

- Do talk about the problem with your child, however. Reassure him/her that a lot of people have difficulty in learning to read and some people take longer to learn things than others but it is nothing to worry about. Bring out those things which your child can do well and let her or him know how proud you are of all their other achievements. Say how especially proud you are of the way your child is trying to master something that she/he finds difficult when other people might be tempted just to give up. Stress that it is not a problem that has to be faced alone – you are going to help and so is his school.
- Always be positive and give lots of praise and encouragement for any effort at all. Don't be afraid to give little treats as rewards, for example: "Gosh, you did try hard today didn't you? I'm so pleased with you that you can have an extra five minutes play before bed time/ an extra comic at the weekend/etc." This is NOT the same as offering a bribe which should be avoided. Give rewards *after* something has been done (but not every time!) Don't say things like "If you've learned to read by the end of the year then I'll buy you a bike." Not only is that such a big goal to achieve that the child is likely to think it is impossible but the very anxiety to succeed which promises like this could bring about may actually make things worse.
- *Never* be negative and say things like "I can't understand why you can't do it." or "Come on, you must know what that is." All that will ever do is to add fuel to your child's worries. If he *could* do it he *would* do it.
- Make sure that everyone in the family treats the child in the same positive and encouraging way and keep a watchful eye and a listening ear on brothers and sisters to make sure there is no teasing, fun-poking or whatever going on. Don't simply think to yourself "Oh my children wouldn't do that!" They are quite likely

to do it even if it is only in the heat of a childish squabble about something else.

- It is particularly hard for the child with reading difficulties to have brothers and sisters who can read well – especially as quite often happens if the brother or sister is younger. For your child's sake, do make sure that any reading to you or helping at home sessions don't take place in front of brothers or sisters. Even though this is difficult to arrange it should be done.
- Some children with reading difficulties start to have behaviour problems or tantrums as a result of their, probably unexpressed, frustration with themselves. This is when you need the patience of a saint. Shouting or retaliating is not going to help the child even if it does make you feel better. Try to understand how very frustrated your child's failure is making her or him feel and bear in mind that they haven't got the self control of an adult. This is not to say that you should let them get away with anti-social behaviour, rather that you should deal with it when you are both feeling calm and you can speak to your child quietly and firmly.
- Finally, remember at all times that your child didn't *choose* to have reading problems and no matter how he or she may appear on the surface your child will be unhappy about it. Give her or him all the support, understanding and encouragement a child like this needs and deserves from a parent.

Schools provision for children for reading problems

There are several Acts of Parliament which govern what happens in schools and one of these is particularly concerned with children with special educational needs. The 1981 Education Act with its accompanying guidelines is exclusively concerned with children with any problem ranging from physical or mental handicap through to any kind of learning difficulty. The act places certain duties on Local Education Authorities as far as the education of such children (who may be as many as 20% of the school population) is concerned. Please note the use of the word *duties* in that sentence for while the act has resulted in improvements and much stronger efforts to meet parents' wishes in most LEAs, the wording of the act is such that not every LEA is sticking to the spirit of the legislation as well as one might wish.

Be that as it may, schools now have a duty to:

- inform parents about any real learning difficulties a child may have
- provide for that child's learning needs either by themselves or by seeking help from an outside agency such as peripatetic remedial teachers from the LEA's service to support children with learning difficulties, or an educational psychologist.

Many primary schools have their own part-time remedial teachers who help with small groups or individual children with reading problems. While such lessons may only take place a couple of times a week, it does mean that individual children receive more individual help than they could normally have in the classroom. Visiting specialist teachers in addition to working with the children also tend to support the class teacher with advice and perhaps materials for use with the children having problems.

Provision does vary from authority to authority around the country. Any questions, worries or concerns you may have should be discussed with your child's headteacher. They will know what provision is available and whether or not extra help is a possibility.

How to get help for your child

First of all be sure that you are not worrying unnecessarily. Your child may simply be developing a little more slowly than you might wish but is, nevertheless, making good steady progress. If, however, you really are convinced that your child has a reading problem and if the school does not appear to be doing anything about it, then you could try the following:

- Ask for an appointment to see the headteacher about your child's reading. That will allow the head time to gather any information about your child's reading from the classteacher.
- When you meet, say how worried you are and ask if there is a visiting specialist teacher who could be asked to come into the school and assess your child's reading.
- Don't be put off by comments about it being a waste of time or that it taking ages for your child to be seen. Even if that is true, the quicker the person is contacted then the quicker your child is likely to be seen.
- If there is no such teacher, then ask if your child can be referred to an educational psychologist. Educational psychologists are specialists in children's learning difficulties and are able to make suggestions as to how a child's needs may best be met. They do tend to have a lot of children referred to them so it may take a while for your child to be seen.
- In the unlikely event that the headteacher refuses to refer your child to an outside agency, take the matter into your own hands. Telephone the Education Authority and ask to speak to someone who can give you advice as to how to have your child's reading difficulties assessed. You can usually find the number listed under the city or county council Education Department.

I think my child might be dyslexic. . .

In order to say a child is dyslexic we need to Know what is meant by the term and here we run into trouble because the word is used to mean different things and to describe a whole range of reading problems.

People sometimes talk about 'word blindness' instead of dyslexia. This is not very helpful because it simply is not true. Many people, including teachers and officials of Local Education Authorities, do not use the word dyslexia and so are sometimes accused of denying that the 'condition' exists. Again this is not true; they simply prefer the use of the term 'specific learning difficulty.'

Whether or not dyslexia or specific learning difficulty is used, it usually refers to children who have severe problems with reading and writing despite having received good classroom teaching. There are those who would say that the main feature of dyslexia is that it cannot be totally cured, only alleviated and dyslexics will have continuing difficulty with reading and writing tasks and related activities as new demands are placed upon them. In other words, the ten year old dyslexic can be taught to cope at his level but will need further support in later years, for example when facing the more sophisticated reading and writing requirements of the sixteen year old.

Diagnosing dyslexia is not something for parents to do, or even for the average classroom teacher if it comes to that. The child who is suspected of having a specific learning difficulty needs to be seen by an educational psychologist or other specialist. It is possible to pay for private assessments at regional Dyslexia Institutes in various parts of the country. This is expensive and you can often get just as good a service from the local educational authority psychologist. If not, then it is worth ontacting the Dyslexia Institute – if there is one close to you.

If your child *is* dyslexic then he or she is going to need some special teaching and whoever does the assessment will be able to advise you on that. There are also a couple of helpful books available if you want to know more and these are mentioned on page 63.

What can I do to help my child?

If you can spare the time, keep cheerful and keep patient there is a lot that you can do which will supplement any extra help he or she is getting in school – or take the place of any help which should be available and isn't for some reason. The following suggestions are all worthwhile but the first six are especially important.

1 Make sure you talk to your child's class teacher. Ask his/her advice about the things you are doing and see what suggestions are forthcoming as to how you can help at home. I can give only general advice in a book – your child's classteacher or remedial teacher can be much more specific.

2 Keep in mind all the advice on page 58 about encouraging your child, boosting confidence and praising all his efforts.

3 Spend time reading to your child. Your child needs to keep alive the idea that stories and reading can be enjoyable even if reading them for himself seems a bit daunting for the time being. Time spent sharing and enjoying books with you is time spent building his motivation to read.

4 Do try the paired reading technique outlined on page 29. If you would really like to go into this in more detail then you will find a book recommended at the end of this one.

5 Do encourage your child to read to you every day for a short while, following the advice on page 26. There will be days when he doesn't want to perhaps, so you read to him first and then let him read it after you.

6 If there *are* days when he doesn't want to have anything to do with reading, then leave it. Don't force him to do it – it's just not worth it.

7 The technique of Look, Cover, Write, Check described on page 49 can also be used to help children build up a sight vocabulary of high frequency words which the child is finding difficult to learn. (Words like: are, who, then, what, they, there, was, because, this, where, like, were, have, done, went, that, etc.) When it is used for reading as well as spelling it is essential that the child says the word each time it is written.

8 As a change, why not make some home-made reading materials together – good for writing as well. You could try:

- a joke poster: a big blank sheet of paper on which the family write and perhaps draw their favourite jokes for your child. Keep them short and fairly simple such as:
  Q: What do you call someone who steals meat?
  A: A hamburglar.
  Q: What's purple and has wrinkles?
  A: A worried grape.
  Q: What is green and goes up and down?
  A: A pea in a lift.
  Q: What is green and goes at 60 mph?
  A: A pea on a motor bike.

  You'll find lots more in, for example, *The Crack A Joke Book* published by Puffin – which is great for shared reading!

- to make a reading book all about your family using a scrapbook and family photographs. Let your child choose the photos to stick in, decide what he wants to say about each one and then write or copy it under the

photo. You could build up the book by doing one or two each night and getting your child to read the previous sentences before he does the new ones.

9 Here's a good reading game to help your child learn certain words. Get him to cut up about twenty pieces of cardboard into squares measuring about two inches. On the squares write ten words which he is not sure about or which he gets muddled on – each word written on two cards. Then turn all the cards face down so that you can't see the words and give them a shuffle around. Then take it in turns to turn over two cards to see if you have got a pair. (Make sure you read the words aloud as you go and try and get your child to join in with you.) If you are careful about not moving the cards, you soon begin to remember where certain cards are and can go for pairs which you then keep. The winner is the one with the most pairs at the end of the game. Do make sure that your child wins more often than you do, won't you?!

Some recommended books

Further information for parents:

The Good Book Guide to Children's Books (for children aged 0–15) Penguin
Helping Children Read, The Paired Reading Handbook by Dr Rober Morgan, Methuen
The Read Aloud Handbook by Jim Trelease, Penguin
More Help For Dyslexic Children by T.R. & Elaine Miles, Methuen
Reading Through Play by Carol Baker, Macdonald

Magazines about books:

Books For Your Children   3 issues per year, annual subscription approx. £2.50 available from 90, Gillhurst Road, Harborne, Birmingham 17
Growing Point   6 issues per year, annual subscription approx. £4.00 available from Ashton Manor, Ashton, Northants NN7 2JL

Some recommended books to share with young children . . .

Unless otherwise stated, these books are all paperback editions.

Nursery Rhymes:
The Mother Goose Treasury by Raymond Briggs, Puffin
Helen Oxenbury Nursery Rhyme Book Heinemann (Hardback)
Over The Moon: A Book Of Nursery Rhymes by Charlotte Voake, Walker (Hardback)
This Little Puffin by Elizabeth Matterson, Puffin

ABC Books:
The Most Amazing Hide-And-Seek Alphabet by Robert Crowther, Viking Kestrel (Hardback)
Lucy and Tom's abc by Shirley Hughes, Puffin
Dr Seuss' ABC Book Collins
Bangers and Mash ABC Book by Paul Groves, Longman

A pick of the paperbacks for young children to share with you . . .

Peepo by Janet and Alan Ahlberg, Picture Puffin
Dear Zoo by Rod Campbell, Picture Puffin
Meg and Mog Books by Nicholl and Pienkowski, Picture Puffin
Old Mother Hubbard by Colin and Jacqui Hawkins, Magnet
Ten, Nine, Eight by Molly Bang, Picture Puffin
Not Now, Bernard by David McKee, Sparrow
The Elephant and the Bad Baby by Vipont and Briggs, Picture Puffin
My Cat Likes To Hide In Boxes by Eve Sutton, Picture Puffin
A House Is a House For Me by Mary Ann Hoberman, Picture Puffin
Wilberforce stories by Margaret Gordon, Picture Puffin
Spot Books by Eric Hill, Picture Puffin
Snowball Books by Helen Piers, Magnet
The Giant Jam Sandwich by John Vernon Lord, Piccolo Picture Books
I to to nursery school by Fiona Prafoff, Magnet
The Great Big Enormous Turnip bu Tolstoy and Oxenbury, Piccolo Picture Books
The Snowman by Raymond Briggs, Picture Puffin
Bear's Room, No Peeping by Michelle Cartlidge, Magnet
The Creepy Crawly Caterpillar by H.E. Todd, Picture Corgi
The Very Hungry Caterpillar by Eric Carle, Picture Puffin
King Rollo books by David McKee, Sparrow Books
Each Peach, Pear, Plum by Janet and Allan Ahlberg, Picture Lion